John Mason

Dives and Lazarus

John Mason

Dives and Lazarus

ISBN/EAN: 9783743344914

Manufactured in Europe, USA, Canada, Australia, Japa

Cover: Foto ©ninafisch / pixelio.de

Manufactured and distributed by brebook publishing software
(www.brebook.com)

John Mason

Dives and Lazarus

INTRODUCTORY.

In an old book (the property of Daniel Deane, an English schoolmaster, who came to this country in 1770), is the original from which this beautiful little work is republished. Having received an education in his native country, Professor Deane was undoubtedly a welcome settler among the pioneers of Western Maryland, where he followed his profession and distinguished himself as a teacher; and near Mount Savage, in Allegany county (where his ashes have rested since A.D. 1805), family descendants and grateful recollections of Schoolmaster Deane are still in existence. For three-quarters of a century this old work has occupied the shelf in the log cabin as well as the book-case of modern times; passing into the possession of the fifth generation, only minus title pages and bearing the imprint that time ever makes on all created things. And when we consider the circumstances through which this ancient relic has existed to the present time, we are constrained to believe that there is something providential in its preservation. During the last four years it has been diligently circulated among the clergy and laity of different denominations with the hope of obtaining an knowledge of the author. One says it sounds like Bunyan's writings; another says it came from Shakespeare.

A Roman Catholic, well learned in ancient Church history, says that "Dives and Lazarus" was written before sects and denominations had an existence in the world. As to the true authorship, we are compelled to leave the reader in total darkness; notwithstanding, it is certainly most gratifying to every true believer (as well as a fearful warning to unbelief) that this sublime production of ancient times has come to light when the infidelity and strange doctrines of the nineteenth century are demanding the stubborn proofs and miraculous manifestations that the rich man in hell required of Abraham in heaven for the salvation of his five brethren. May the God of Israel impress upon the hearts of the readers the unchangeable truth of His words, the surety of His promises, and the justice of His judgments.

DIVES AND LAZARUS.

LUKE, XVI: 19—31.

In Judah's vale a man of wealth abode,
Vile as a beast, yet worship'd as a God ;
Who Tyrian cloaths, and Egypt's linen wore,
And on whose table met land, sea and air.
Beneath the threshold of his outmost gate
A pale, deformed, horrid carcase sat ;
Another Job, but of more fixed woes,
Who from his dunghill never once arose.

*God help me was his Name. God was his all.
Those few that knew him, Lazarus did him call.

Need, Pains and Scorn, at once did on him lie ;
His bed was earth, his covering was the sky.
Nothing had he to pay off nature's scores,
Empty he was of bread, but full of sores.

*The English of Lazarus.

Hunger (that rack) will make a man confess
What modest minds endeavour to suppress.
Sharp Hunger whets the wit, and mends its Strain.
It hurts the Bowels, but it helps the Brain.
A servant pass'd the gate, where lo! he found
This rueful object grov'ling on the ground.
Said Lazarus, Sir, if pity be my due,
Give to your master what I give to you.

LAZARUS *his Petition*.

Most noble Sir, I humbly crave
What nature doth expect of me;
I am a borderer on the grave
Half slain with sharp necessity.

For childrens bread I do not call;
I do not ask thy servants fare;
Only the Sweeping of thy hall
I beg and what your Dogs may spare.

Doom me not, Sir, to perish at your gate,
Who may preserve me at so cheap a rate,
For farther Judah's sake some fragments give,
I'll serve you at God's altars whilst I live.

Dives *his Answer*.

WHAT dog is this that dares presume on me?
Accurst be all such crawling toads as he,
Pests of my gate, vermin that creep so nigh,
———— I hate 'em; let him rot and die.

In vain the poor man's thoughts persu'd his Suit,
The dogs were humane, but their Lord a brute,
They left their snarling to their Master's face;
They ran, and Lazarus gently did embrace.
He was the pity'd patient of those hounds,
Whose lambent tongues did cool his burning
    wounds.

This done, the squalid vassals of the times
Scorn'd ragged virtue, honour'd purple crimes,
Things are mis-judged by the purblind eye,
Which views their posture, not their tendency,
'Till Justice wakes to right its injur'd laws,
Which doth not weigh the person but the cause.

Nor rags, nor sores, are clouds that can dis-
    guise,
A splendid soul of Heaven's, soul searching
    Eyes;

Earth's Laz'rus was Heav'ns; Dives earth's
    disdain,
Was a meet guest for Heaven to entertain,
Now comes the golden hour that sets him free,
From his Apprenticeship to misery.
His corps (the Grave's old neighbour) long
    undrest,
At length is slipt into its bed of rest,
A treasure 'tis tho' Funeral cost it wants;
The richest mineral is the dust of saints:
He was his own (most serious) mourner here;
He mourn'd enough, he needs no hired tear.

    The time is come that Lazarus must be clad,
With such fine linen Dives never had,
The time is come that Lazarus must be fed
With Heaven's rich juices, and with Angels
    Bread.

    There is a table richly spread above,
There is an everlasting Feast of love;
A Feast which Friends and Friendship doth
    maintain.
Pale envy is not there, nor proud disdain;

They are all in one, in one they all agree
One is their all, which makes all one to be,
Here's height of mirth with depth of seriousness,
Plenty without the hazard of excess;
Here are full joys in hand, full joys in view,
Here wine and appetite are ever new;
Ever begins their feast and ne'er doth end,
Whom growing loaves and living springs attend;
Their Harps are well strung Hearts, well-tuned
    Tongues;
And sacred Hallelujahs are their Songs;
Here sit the saints, here the Believers Sire
Is nobly seated in his rich Attire;
Hither the King of Heaven new Guests does call
Nor can he come too late that comes at all.

The mighty one who dwells and rules on high,
Angels attend with an obedient Eye.
The Secrets of his Breast they do not Skill,
But are the trusty Servants of his Will.

  Thus charg'd he them, ' bring Lazarus to the
    Feast,
'And let him take his place next Abraham's
    Breast,'

They heard with rev'rence, and obeyed their
    King,
Joy rais'd their hearts, and nimbly shook their
    Wing.
They fled from heaven, yet heaven was with
    them still,
It was their heaven to do their masters will.
They stopt not at the stars that pompous show
Who went to view a brighter star below.
The point design'd they well did understand,
Who had old Voy'gers been to Canaan's land.
There had they been Lot's guests [who was
    their ward.]
There had they been Elisha's flaming guard,
In that land chiefly lay their Lord's affairs,
They that traffick'd there for souls [those pre-
    cious Wares]
Soon came they where sick Lazarus had his
    Lare,
They stopp'd and waited for their passenger;
No visitant found they with him but the
    Lord,
No nurse but faith, no cordial but the word.

They heard him praying, 'Lord, some mercy
    shew
' For I cant find no mercy here below.'

  This said, he sigh'd, and was of life bereav'd,
He gave his soul, and they his soul receiv'd ;
With Shouts and songs triumphant up they went,
And to the company did him present ;
They shouted all, and joy'd the new come guest,
He gently stoops, and leans on Abraham's Breast,
    Whom Dives curs'd and stately fools dis-
      dain'd,
How is he bless'd ! how is he entertain'd !
Tho' virtue here on earth neglected lies ;
Yet heaven will raise it, for 'tis born to rise.
Dives, that silken God must never die,
Unless his creatures and false prophets lie,
He's safe, if death he casts as far behind
His body, as it is below his mind.
He's always young, he learns it from his glass,
Which smoothes his furrow'd brow and paints
    his face.
But a cold striking hand confutes the lye;
Down falls his flattering glass, his fancies die ;

His Garden-walks must him no longer know,
The life tree in his garden doth not grow
His Palace must be chang'd for a dark tomb;
That was his inn, but this must be his home;
He must no longer at his table stay,
The voider (death) is come to take away :
Death, that abhorr'd (both name and) thing,
　　comes on,
And potently torments this potent one :
It makes amazing breaches; and, in short,
Hath seized the out work and attacks the fort,
In what a wretched posture does he lie!
He cannot live, and yet he dares not die.
His Debt must be distrain'd; for he'll not pay,
Nor yield his Ghost; it must be fetched away,
He spurns, he struggles, but Death keeps him
　　under,
And with one Stroke tears flesh and Soul
　　asunder;
Then rang the house with his five Bretherns
　　Cries;
Alas! Our Brother! so they closed his Eyes,
His outward Parts are wash'd his inner Rooms
Stuffed with *Arabian* Sweets and rich Perfumes

Now Death his Purple is, now he's allow'd,
Fine Linen too, but 'tis a Fun'ral shroud;
Gravefac'd Spectators with their garments
     torn
And shrouded Lips attend, the Room doth
     mourn.
Ah what a poor Revenge is this on fate!
For one that cannot live, to lie in State.
Amidst the gazing Croud the Bearers come,
With Pomp they bring him to his painted
     Tomb.
Minstrels and Trumpeters their Noises join,
And Women sell false Tears for current Coin.
Now lest his Friends should in salt Streams be
     drown'd,
The Cup of Consolation goes its Round.
But stay, my Soul, 'tis Death that thou must
     view,
Not Shadows which dead Bodies do ensue.

   What a dark Notion and Absurdity
Is this to living Men that they must die!
Grim death on his pale horse triumphant rides,
He strikes us thro' our nearest kinsman's sides.

Yet are we senseless as the stupid mule,
Live as exceptions from the common rule;
We cast a cloth o'er death, 'tis soon forgot;
We charm the serpent, and it stings us not.

Now might one let this pleasant error pass,
If death was all: but death his second has:
When once the dissolution-hour is come,
Out goes the soul to hear her final doom.

You who have slightly heard the fun'ral knell,
Now hear the voice which dooms the soul to
    Hell;
For those whose hearts an Earthquake will not
    shake,
Tho' heaven's loud roaring cannon may awake.

Dives black ghost (all horror and despair)
Is from its prison snatch'd to th' dismal bar:
Behind him the impatient devils roar,
His sins (those worst of devils) stand before;
With terrors thus besieg'd in every Place,
He hears a voice, but might not see the face.
The voice was thunder roaring in his ears,
The word were tearing bolts and flaming spears;

"Go, thou accurst, vile caitif, hence away
" To damned Ghosts: come devils take your
    Prey."
Struck with this thunder down he sunk he fell
And was a triumph to the fiends of hell.
Th' ingenious tyrants did a council pack,
Their malice sets their wits upon the rack.
When they had jointly study'd to torment,
For their pale prisoner then in haste they sent
They chain'd and stak'd him to a furious flame
Where constant Streams of brimstone feed the
    same.
Behold sin's martyr, and hell's sacrifice!
He yells and howls, and vents unpity'd cries.
He finds no friendly ear or tender eye,
He feels a thousand deaths, but cannot die;
Like burning brass, he's fir'd in every part,
A vulture lives upon his living heart.
God's gone, he's gone, and what an hell is this
To be deprived of everlasting bliss!
O this eternal banishment is worse,
Than all the remnant of the doom's day curse.
This hell of hell may thus be understood,
No torments are so bad as God is good.

Besides, an appetite in Man doth lie,
Which nothing but a God can satisfy;
And tho' his appetite be here deluded
By various objects in God's room obtruded,
Yet when at death all these are laid aside,
Then thirsts the soul for God, but is deny'd;
This thirst unquench'd is such an inward
        flame
And hell in hell is its deserved name;
In hell their cannot be an atheist,
    'Tis hell in hell that God is dearly mist.
Poor Dives cries, " the God for whom I starve
" I cannot see, because I would not serve;
" I bleed to think, [and thinking is my fate]
" He often knocked at my bolted gate,
" Where are those baits on which my lusts did
        prey,
" The price for which I cast myself away?
" Where's now my pomp and pride, my fests
        and sports,
" Whose chains detain'd me from the sacred
        courts?
"O did my house so near the temple stand!
"O did I perish out of Judah's Land!

" Might I be betray'd once more ! but 'tis too
    late,

" Justice hath lock'd the golden mercy-gate.

" Now I believe and tremble; I repent,

" But my repentance is my punishment.

" It is not virtue, but necessity ;

"Alas ! how miserably wise am I ?

" Might I return now to that happy night,

" Which veil'd me ere my parent saw the light;

"Ah me ! must I lie here, and ne'er came out."

He raves and flings his curses round about.

He curs'd both hea'vn and hell, he curs'd the
    Earth,

He curs'd the day that witness'd to his birth :

But neither can his tears his griefs assauge,

Nor does it cool his heart to vent his rage.

This keen reflection makes the furnace glow,

" It must be ever with me as 'tis now.

" Hell's flames no ashes will produce : but I

" Must ever dying live, and living die.

" Souls for themselves the balm of patience
    bear ;

" 'Tis the poor's physick, but it grows not here.

" My soul is filled with home-bred tears and
  taunts;

" 'Tis its own fury, and itself it haunts.

" Pity was wont in misery's house to dwell,

" But I am haled by the hounds of hell.

" Time us'd to be a surgeon good at wounds;

" But I am got beyond its happy bounds.

"A vessel charg'd with scalding wrath am I,

" Hoop'd in the circle of eternity."

You who affect the pleasant path to hell,
And love damnation in its causes well,
Look straight before you on your journey's
  end,
Do ye not see th' infernal smoak ascend?
Have not the sparks into your bosom flown.
Whereby the neighb'ring coasts may well be
  known?
Bold sinner, stop, no further progress make,
Lest your next step be in the firey lake;
But Oh! he redicules his soul's affairs,
And labours to be damn'd at unawares.
His humour would not bear a countermand;
Alas for them who hate to understand!

Who on their souls experiments will try,
At the charge of a sad eternity.
Alas for them who never will awake
Till they are plung'd into the burning lake.

Dives was here struck blind with flattering lyes,
Now the hell-brand lifts up his flaming eyes,
He spies the region where the happy dwell,
But heaven at distance is another hell.
He spies a Canaan's feast; for chiefly there
The natives of his country do appear :
He spies blest Abraham with his faithful race,
And Lazarus sitting next to Abraham's place.
Oh ! how it twinges and torments his eyes ?
His scorn to envy turns, and thus he cries;
" The scoundrel who lay starving at my gate,
" Is now a peer in heaven, and Angel's mate ;
" The beggar sits and feeds on Angel's fare,
" His rags are robes, such as heav'ns nobles
        wear;
" The dog, whom in derision once I had,
" Is turn'd into a star, which makes me mad."
Now Dives is a beggar, and applies
Himself to Abraham with his mournful cries.

DIVES *his Petition.*

AH! Father Abraham pity me,
Who with tormenting flames am stung,
For pity whether should I flee,
But to the bowels whence I sprung?
The Grapes rich blood I do not crave,
Waters cheap element will suffice;
And tho' my tongue thirsts for a wave,
For one poor drop it only cries.
By Lazarus moist'ned finger may you please
To give my scorched tongue one moment ease.
I dwell in flames, and flames in me do dwell;
O for a drop from heaven to sweeten hell.

Mark how the wheel is turn'd, the time is come
He begs a drop, who once deny'd a crumb.
Right thinking Judges then must need aprove,
The tart and equal answer from above.

ABRAHAM's *Answer.*

ART thou forlorn of God and com'st to me,
What can I tell thee then but misery?
Remember, son, the Heav'n, thy feet have trod,
Earth was thy Heav'n, and pleasure was thy God.

Remember *Lazarus* had his hell below,
Thou wert the devil which did cause his woe;
Now are his rags Heav'n's robes with glorious
    beams,
Thy purple, flames, thy junkets, sulph'rous
    Streams.

Is he thy wish who was thy scorn before?
Shall *Lazarus* now be welcome to thy door?
And dost imagine some fair bridge to lie
Between the white and black eternity?
No, there's a mighty gulf which rends in twain
The fiery region and the etherial plain.
We are too happy to be dispossest,
And you so cursed, you can ne'er be blest;
We are so rais'd that we can never fall,
And you so sunk, you cannot raise at all,
Once Angels went from heaven to hell; but
    first
They blackened were to devils and accur'st;
Since those stars fell, none of the heaven'ly host
Or did, or shall, visit the Infernal coast.
To you 'tis bitter; but to us 'tis sweet,
That we are parted, and must never meet:

Heav'n were not heav'n, if it near hell was
    plac'd,
Nor hell were no hell, if it of heav'n might
    taste.
Can our pure light with smoak and darkness
    dwell,
The poles shall sooner meet than heaven and
    hell.
  Though speech avails not, racking misery
  Extorts from him another fruitless cry.

DIVES *his Second Petition.*

If such an envious gulph there be,
Yet father, lend an ear to me,
From earth to heaven away is paved:
How else came Lazarus to be saved?
Let me so small a boon entreat,
That Lazarus may his steps repeat.
And that he may embody'd go,
And tell the stories of my woe
To my five bretheren who all dwell within
My father's house (Oh ! had we never been,
Brethern in bond of nature and of sin.)

O let him tell them that there is a God,
Whose sceptre is a sin-revenging rod;
And let him tell them that adventurous drolls
Shall find unto their cost that they have souls.
Mine stuck i' th' scabbard till its angry Lord
Unsheathed it, and proved a flaming sword.
That limbeck, death, draws spirits from our Clay
To the element of souls they haste away;
And let him tell them that the Sadducee
Shall be hell's convert, and recant with me;
Whilst they lie sleeping on the brink of hell.
The smoak they see not, nor the brimstone
        smell;
There they'll disport themselves with golden
        Dreams,
Till they betray 'em to these burning streams;
But let him scare them with an hollow sound,
That they [like Lot] may flee the curs'd ground.
O send him quickly; lest they tumble in,
And prove the flaming records of my sin:
Can I no water get at my desire?
Yet, O! no more, no more new flakes of fire.

This Abraham heard with unrelenting ears;
No Pity's due to hell-hounds cries and tears.

Abraham *his Answer*.

Once heav'n bow'd down and touched th'
    Arabian hill,
And gave a sample of the sacred will
To Mose's hands that chosen man of God,
Copies were taken, and dispers'd abroad.
    So his kind arms abroad the river flings,
    So the free sun extends his fruitful wings;
    As this most sacred light itself displays,
    And gilds the tents of Jacob with its rays.
For saints to come from God there is no cause,
Himself came down, and did promulge his laws
Need Lazarus take a Journey from the sky,
When wisdom at your bretherns gates doth cry,
Let them hear Moses, read by their divines
I'th' synagogue, to which their house adjoins;
And let them hear the reverend prophets next,
Those wond'rous commentators on the text.

Dives *his Reply*.

Moses ['tis true] was an unerring guide,
So were those Sixteen prophets on his Side?
This I as much believe as if I saw
The flaming mount and heard the firey law,

When every word was accented with thunder,
Which rent those oaks the Jewish hearts
    asunder:
'Tis here as necessary to believe,
As it is natural to feel and grieve.
I that am now a proof of sacred writ:
Do argue backwards with my after wit,
Hell in the threatnings tho' I did not see,
The threatnings are in Hell made plain to me,
I skowl'd upon the Heavens when they did
    lowre
The Clouds I fear'd not, but I feel the Shower.
Nothing will move my brethren but a Sign,
Experience is the powerfullest divine :
Faith is the child of sense whereas report
Is entertain'd with Blasphemy or Sport :
They have a Sword to cut the Gordian Knot
Moses *saith many things, but proves them not.*
And tho' they hear substantial proofs there be,
Nothing is proof to them but what they see.
Had they an emissary from above,
The very sight a future state would prove ;
Might he but tell them of your heavenly strand
They'd all turn pilgrims for that holy land :

Or might he preach the torments which I feel
His word would wound like burning gads of Steel;
His word would tear down all, like thund'ring
    Guns,
Beyond the faint attemps of Levi's sons.
    O were I of this cursed chain releas'd !
[With that he gnash'd his teeth, and knock'd
    his breast :]
Might I be to the earth a Preacher sent,
I'd burn up sin like stubble where I went ;
I'd smoke away their lusts and flattering lyes,
Or forth I'd drive them with my glaring eyes.
I'd blow a trumpet which should rend the
    Ground,
Their trembling heart-strings should in consort
    sound :
I'd teach the faithless Saducees their creed,
And make the Pharisees to pray indeed ;
I'd tell the Ranters such a doleful tale,
That they should mourn as in Megiddo's vale ;
I'd unbewitch the sots and slaves of sin,
That such a reformation should begin,
As in Josiah's time did not befall,
And the next age should canonize them all.

ABRAHAM'S *Rejoinder.*

A PREACHING apparition would confound
Heaven-daring Giants with its dreadful sound;
None quake so soon as they who heaven do dare
Who fear not God, the greatest cowards are :
But where the coast once clear, the shake once
    o'er,
The lees would settle as they did before.
   It was a walking dream they would conclude
   A Juggle which our senses did delude,
   Or did we something see? and something
     hear?
Yet whence it came it doth not yet appear.
Nay, they would gravely reason out the case,
" What we can grasp we gladly will embrace,
" The rest we leave : to them let children hark
" And fright themselves with fancies in the dark
" What is a spirit? what's infinity?
" What does the word [eternal] signify?"
Charmed are their souls with this oration made
And now their fear shall vanish like the shade.
Thus fools [tho' pounded] will not lose a grain,
And frozen snakes, when thaw'd will hiss again.

Come now thou that pretend'st to act the man,
Something there needs must be which ne'er
     began;
If all were nothing once, so 'twould be now,
A number from bare cyphers could not grow.
Athing's a barren womb: if that could breed,
To be, and not to be were well agreed.
One point is gain'd that something ever was:
This hard word ever you must let it pass.
Know'st thou how far this ever doth extend?
You must grant what you cannot comprehend
But what was ever? this imperial robe
Suits not the azur nor the verdant globe.
One is a turning wheel that spins out Time,
The other Pools with Spots of harden'd Slime.
Now mark the Kinds of each, and you shall find
Unto their proper Spheres they are confin'd.
Hereby is their Original confest,
There's but a partial goodness in the best.
This is the Voice of their Infirmity,
' *Meer beggars and Derivatives are we.*'
What's of itself that doth itself suffice,
'Tis from our Creatureship our wants arise,

What of itself, that in itself is blest,
'Tis its own Center and a perfect Rest;
Rich is that Being whence all Beings are,
And whence each Being hath its proper Share,
Nor is't a wonder of so high Degree,
To make to be, as of itself to be;
Something then ever was, which needs must
    be,
From all the shades of imperfections free.
Hence are we; and to think, in vain we are,
Is to condemn his wisdom at our Bar.
As men the badge of their dependence wear
On their frail flesh, (the grave's probationer,)
And on their hearts, whose restless motions
    show
Something they want, which is not here below;
So must they own whom they are forced to
    know
And pay themselves to whom themselves they
    owe.
Neither would this Light of Comfort dim,
But they should serve themselves in serving
    him.

When Graves upbraid proud Grave-stones with
    their Lyes,
God's Servant is a Title never dies.
The thoughts in man do prove his Soul to be,
His conscience bodes his Immortality.
This bosom Magistrate his facts espies,
And binds him over to the last assize.
He trembles at his summons to appear ;
His fear makes not a God, God makes his fear,
RELIGION by corroding, doth assay
Even thro' an heart of rock to force its way.
O might he to himself be so sincere,
To strive to please whom he's constrain'd to
    fear !
  Yet will he be a vagrant all his days,
Without a method to direct his ways.
What eye er'e pierc'd th' Almighty's sacred
    breast ?
Himself knows only what will please him best.
Since man was made to serve his Maker's will,
Which is an height transcending human skill ;
A rule must needs be granted from on high
For him to regulate his actions by.

This Heaven-sprung rule that sacred-roll con-
    tains,
Which in the consecrated Land remains,
Its words and mysteries are all Divine,
And weighty mountains hang on every line;
It (Sun like) shines by its own golden beams,
And scorns its base Co-rival senseless Dreams.
Those Spangles which the *Heathen* Sages left,
Were from this Mine snatch'd by an honest
    Theft.
Give me that hardy Brow that dares deny
The Bible's well attested History.
Moses said many things, and prov'd them too,
With proofs, which all hell's magic did outdo.
God's power he carried in his hands to show
That from his mouth the truths of God did
    flow;
And his credentials on his face did shine,
Which there were written by a beam divine.
The gazing jews were struck who plainly saw,
That whence he had his light, he had his law
   Those sections which the sacred code begin
Where by an age of wonders usher'd in.

The Prophets superstructure firmly stands
On two hewn stones laid by th' Almighty's
    hands.
They count the footsteps of their coming Lord
They view the mercy seat with one accord.
One tells his name, another tells his place
Another rites the beauties of his face.
Thus as he glanced at by their piercing eyes,
The last of them is harbinger espies.
And O the brisk the charming Airs that spring
From the consent of each harmonious string!
He's overwise who dreads fictitious lines
From hands unbrib'd, and hearts without de-
    signs.
They wrote beyond themselves, which serves
    to prove,
Their hearts and hands were guided from above.
The world's just age, and what was done of Old,
Are in the sacred register enroll'd.
Here may be seen the pristine state of man,
And, [that nile's head] the source where Ills
    began,
Here may be seen what makes a second spring
Here is the best account of every thing.

The wonders witness now by mortal eyes,
Are but the products of its prophesies.

The Scriptures rule the world : till this shall
    burn,
All ages on the axle-tree shall turn.

This heaven inspired volume doth avow,
What reason may embrace or must alow.
When God describes himself, 'tis such an Height,
As far surmounts quick fancy's highest flight.
'Tis reason, reason should be puzzled here
Man should be God, if he knew what he were.
To these vast heights thus sober reason saith,
I see the seals and yield the chair to faith.
Now the Almighty's word shall vermin slight,
When Heaven and earth bear witness to his
    Might ?
Vast numbers from his word did flow,
And must his word pass for a cypher now ?
Nay, his commands at first creations were,
And now his word commands and gives an ear
It is a sun that gives both light and eyes,
A voice that bids, and makes the dead arise

It makes clouds, stars, and sends them to the
    Sky,
And turneth heaven into a colony.
Unbelief is not reason, but a lust;
God's hand and sword give it its mortal thrust.
The Law of the two Tables will prevail,
When other (self-invented) Means shall fail.
Whilst other Archers level in the Dark,
The arrows from God's Quiver hit the mark.
What Voices or what Visions, would you have?
God's Voice (or nothing) will your Brethern
    save.
New Methods of Salvation to contrive,
Is fruitless Labour; let 'em hear and live:
But if they won't, their *Mittimus* is sealed;
A stubborn Patient never can be heal'd.

If Preachers rais'd by God they will disdain,
Preachers rais'd from the Grave would preach in
    vain.

FINIS.

TRUE WISDOM.

In this progressive age (as the world terms it) we fail to understand or realize that the wonderful accomplishments of the present day are the legitimate productions of toiling millions through centuries of time's undevastating flight. Each succeeding generation and individual, from Adam to the present age, have contributed their span of toil and experience to the grand attainments of the nineteenth century. The menial apprenticeship and alphabet of letters and figures are the legitimate rudimentary principles from which the mechanic and scholar attained to distinction, honor and fame. The sturdy, towering majestic oak of the forest had its humble origin in the apparently worthless and simple acorn; all nature and experience ever teaching the faithful yet unobserved lessons of elementary principle, system, and progressive growth.

How wide the contrast in the progress of science and religion. The population of the world is supposed to be over twelve hundred millions, and their religions have been approximated as follows:

Christians, - - - -	353,000,000
Buddhists, - - - -	483,000,000
Brahmmists, - - - -	120,000,000
Mohammedans, - - -	120,000,000
Parsees, - - - - -	1,000,000
Jews, - - - -	8,000,000
Miscellaneous, Fetish worshipers,	
Atheists, etc., - - -	189,000,000

A glance at the above statistics show that only a little more than one-fourth of the world's population are nominal Christians; and, without attempting to pull the mote out of the eyes of three-fourths of the world with the fingers of one-fourth, let us endeavor to see what we have within the pale of the professing Christian denomination of the earth. Outside of the Roman Catholic, Eastern, or Oriental Churches, there are more than fifty different Protestant church organizations and new sects and denominations still coming into existence, as though religion was a matter of invention or discovery. Behold their different doctrines of faith and forms of worship, each party claiming to be in the narrow path, and all manifesting their belligerent attitudes, bickerings, jealousies and animosities. Try to comprehend the means employed and the results accomplished, and no thoughtful mind will be surprised or dismayed at the indifference, unbelief and infidelity in the evening of the nineteenth century.

Job xxviii: 20, 28.—Whence, then, cometh *wisdom*, and where is the place of understanding, seeing it is hid from the eyes of all living and kept close from the fowls of the air? Destruction and death say, we have heard the fame thereof with our ears. God understandeth the way thereof, and he knoweth the way thereof; for He looketh to the ends of the earth, and seeth under the whole heaven, to make the weight for the winds; and He weigheth the waters by measure, when He made a decree for the rain, and a way for the lightning of the thunder. Then did He see it, and declare it; He prepared it; yea, and searched it out. And unto man He said: Behold, the fear of the Lord—

that is *wisdom;* and to depart from evil is under-standing.

We have evidently commenced at the wrong end of the work, and have undertaken conic sections, calculus and astronomy in spiritual matters before we learned the alphabet of true *wisdom.*

King Solomon, the greatest in *wisdom,* wealth and influence, possessing all the powers of the world (for which the nations of the earth are still toiling, sweating and panting), after searching out, experimenting and testing to his full satisfaction, makes a free and full con-fession (in the Book of Ecclesiasticus), saying all is vanity and vexation of spirit.

Let us hear the conclusion of the whole matter—fear God and keep His *commandments;* for this is the whole duty of man.

Has it ever occurred to your mind that in all of that wonderful book the Bible, the book of books (containing the writings and experiences of the Prophets, Priests, Kings and Evangelists), that the *Ten Commandments* are the only part of that most wonderful work that God Almighty the Father wrote with His own finger in tables of stone, came down from heaven, and, on the beetling brow of a frowning Sinai, gave his orders and directions to man—the alphabet of true *wisdom*—a rule and system to live by. And behold the instructions, warnings, threatenings and promises after the giving of the law.

Deut. iv: 1, 2.—Now, therefore, hearken, O Israel, unto the statutes and unto the judgments which I teach you, for to do them, that ye may live, and go in and possess the land which the Lord God of your fathers

giveth you. Ye shall not add unto the word which
I command you, neither shall ye diminish aught from
it, that ye may keep the *commandments* of the Lord
your God which I command you.

Leviticus xxvi: 3 to 5, 14, 16, 19, 20.—If ye walk in
my statutes, and keep my *commandments*, and do them,
then I will give you rain in due season, and the land
shall yield her increase, and the trees of the field shall
yield their fruit; and your threshing shall reach unto
the vintage, and the vintage shall reach unto the sowing
time; and you shall eat your bread to the full, and
dwell in your land safely; but if ye will not hearken
unto Me, and will not do all these *commandments*, I also
shall do this unto you: I will even appoint over you
terror, consumption, and the burning ague; that I will
consume the eyes, and cause sorrow of heart; and ye
shall sow your seed in vain, for your enemies shall eat
it.   And I will break the pride of your power, and I will
make your heaven as iron, and your earth as brass; and
your strength shall be spent in vain, for your land shall
not yield her increase, neither shall the trees of the land
yield their fruits.

Psalms lxxviii: 5 to 7.—For He established a testi-
mony in Jacob, and appointed a law in Israel, which He
commanded our fathers, that they should make them
known to their children; that the generation to come
might know them, even the children which should be
born, who should arise and declare them to their chil-
dren, that they might set their hope in God, and not
forget the works of God, but keep His *commandments*.

Deut. vi: 6 to 9.—And these words, which I com-
mand thee this day, shall be in thy heart.   And thou

shalt teach them diligently unto thy children, and shalt talk of them when thou sittest in thine house, and when thou walkest by the way, and when thou liest down, and when thou risest up. And thou shalt bind them for a sign upon thine hand, and they shall be as frontlets between thine eyes. And thou shalt write them upon the posts of thy house, and on thy gates.

First Timothy, iii: 5.—For if a man know not how to rule his own house, how shall he take care of the Church of God?

When parents become the preachers and teachers of their own households and home circles, and the *commandments*, the *golden text*, the central subject of their teachings, peace will dwell within their walls, and prosperity within their palaces; and Death, even Death! will be realized as only the opening and closing of the everlasting gates between the Beulah Land and the Celestial City.

THE TEN COMMANDMENTS.

FIRST TABLE.

OUR DUTY TO GOD.

Exodus xx.

I.—THOU shall have no other gods before me.

II.—Thou shalt not make unto thee any graven image, or any likeness of any thing that is in the heaven above, or that is in the earth beneath, or that is in the water under the earth: Thou shalt not bow down thyself to them, nor serve them: for I the Lord thy God am a jealous God, visiting the iniquity of the fathers upon the children unto the third and fourth generation of them that hate me; and shewing mercy unto thousands of them that love me and keep my commandments.

III.—Thou shalt not take the name of the Lord thy God in vain; for the Lord will not hold him guiltless that taketh His name in vain.

IV.—Remember the Sabbath day, to keep it holy: Six days shalt thou labor, and do all thy work: But the seventh day is the Sabbath of the Lord thy God: in it thou shalt not do any work, thou, thy man servant, nor thy maid servant, nor thy cattle, nor thy stranger that is within thy gates: For in six days the Lord made heaven and earth, the sea, and all that in them is, and rested on the Sabbath day; wherefore the Lord blessed the Sabbath day and hallowed it.

SECOND TABLE.

Our Duty to Our Fellow-Man.

V.—Honor thy father and thy mother, that thy days may be long upon the land the Lord thy God giveth thee.

VI.—Thou shalt not kill.

VII.—Thou shalt not commit adultery.

VIII.—Thou shalt not steal.

IX.—Thou shalt not bear false witness against thy neighbor.

X.—Thou shalt not covet thy neighbor's house: thou shalt not covet thy neighbor's wife, nor his man servant, nor his maid servant, nor his ox, nor his ass, nor anything that is thy neighbor's.

———

Since man was made to serve his Maker's will,
Which is an height transcending human skill;
A *rule* must needs be granted from on high,
For him to regulate his actions by.

www.ingramcontent.com/pod-product-compliance
Lightning Source LLC
Chambersburg PA
CBHW032140080426
42733CB00008B/1144